Chris

Todd

Jennifer

Bonseok

Scott

To order additional copies of this book, contact:
Xlibris
844-714-8691
www.Xlibris.com
Orders@Xlibris.com

ISBN:	Softcover	978-1-4257-7387-8
	Hardcover	978-1-4257-7391-5

Library of Congress Control Number: 2007902009

Print information available on the last page

Rev. date: 09/20/2021

The River Edge 9/11 Memorial Gardens

The River Edge 9/11 Memorial Gardens Committee:

Ronald Hardiman

George Riley

James Conway

Ann McCarthy

Scott

Todd

Bonseok

Jennifer

Chris

The River Edge 9/11 Memorial Gardens
Dedicated to the memory of our neighbors
lost in the attack on the
World Trade Center
September 11, 2001.

Christopher Allingham
Jennifer Louise Fialko
Bonseok Koo
Todd Ouida
Scott W. Rohner

Why a garden?

A flower lined path beckons visitors to the south lawn of the River Edge Public Library. Following the path one discovers a garden of remembrance created by a close-knit community of neighbors. There are five private places to rest and reflect on cherished fathers, sons, and a daughter from River Edge who were lost in the attack at the World Trade Center on September 11th, 2001. This is one New Jersey town's response to the evil of that terrible day – to defy death with a living creation of beauty and hope.

Why a garden? The people of River Edge, after recovering from the initial shock following the events of 9/11, rallied to support their neighbors. Indeed, a tide of support in the form of monies and manpower swept through the entire nation. As time passed, the community's need to establish a permanent reminder of that day and to memorialize loved ones lost still remained. Would a plaque or the naming of a structure or other symbolic gesture be enough? What about creating a living entity which would require nurturing and would grow and flourish with the passing years? A visually beautiful place where one could reflect, be comforted, and hopefully refreshed by the surroundings – what about a garden?

Positive ideas become reality when they have the backing of a resolute community. The River Edge 9/11 Memorial Gardens now exist so that the loved ones of those lost can hopefully find some peace. The memorial also acts as a historical reference for future generations of River Edge residents. Created with the assistance of private donations, the memorial speaks of a community that truly cares for each of its members and beckons them to visit, remember and be renewed. Its presence on the grounds of the River Edge Public Library is testament to the belief that freedom of thought and education will triumph over oppression, ignorance and hate.

Garden Development

Following the events of September 11th, 2001, the River Edge community immediately mobilized to assist the town's five families in dealing with the traumatic loss of their loved ones. A committee was formed to coordinate monetary donations from local businesses, religious organizations, area schools and private individuals. These funds were distributed to the five families. The town's educational community recognized the loss of former students Jennifer, Todd and Scott with memorials located on school grounds.

The desire to do more for the families remained. During the winter of 2004, River Edge Library Board members Ronald Hardiman and George Riley approached their board about utilizing the south lawn of the library for a memorial dedicated to the five individuals. With the board's enthusiastic approval, the design stage of the memorial began. Charles Keehn donated the services of his company, Keehn Landscape Contractors, to assist in launching the project. His landscape designer, Patrick A. Smith, prepared several layouts and created a design consisting of a winding garden path where five granite markers and accompanying benches commemorate each of the individuals who perished. The design was presented to the members of the River Edge Borough Council who unanimously gave their approval to the concept.

With the addition of town residents James Conway as treasurer and Ann McCarthy as administrator, the River Edge 9/11 Memorial Gardens Committee was established. The financial goal of the committee was to raise awareness and funds for the project. The borough council agreed to make monies available through the state's Open Space funding allowance. The committee pledged to have the garden completed by September 11th, 2005.

Fundraising activities for the memorial began with a luncheon sponsored by the River Edge Chamber of Commerce and Sanducci's Trattoria of River Edge. A ground-breaking ceremony followed this successful event on September 11th, 2004. During the ceremony a representative from each family spoke, expressing gratitude to the community for the project being undertaken. To symbolize the commencement of the project, two holly bushes were planted by Mayor Margaret Watkins and library board president, George Dunphey.

The bid for construction of the garden was awarded to Let It Grow Incorporated of River Edge. Over the course of the year donations poured into the library from local residents, businesses, and organizations. Additionally, relatives and friends of the five families contributed generously to the project. A list of over six hundred contributors appears in the back of this book. The committee extends its heartfelt thanks to all those who so generously gave of themselves to successfully complete this project.

The River Edge 9/11 Memorial Gardens

Dedication
September 11, 2005

On Sunday, September 11th 2005, the townspeople of River Edge and friends and relatives of the Koo, Allingham, Fialko, Ouida and Rohner families joined together to dedicate the newly constructed River Edge 9/11 Memorial Gardens. The River Edge Police Department Ceremonial Honor Guard and Mayor Margaret Watkins opened the ceremony with a salute to the flag. An interfaith choir, composed of members from various congregations in town, sang the *Star-Spangled Banner*. Scripture readings were given by representatives from St. Peter the Apostle Roman Catholic Church, Grace Lutheran Church, Temple Sholom, First Congregational United Church of Christ and Central Unitarian Church of Paramus. The keynote speaker of the day was River Edge resident, Creighton Drury, who had interviewed each of the five families to most accurately share with the community their thoughts regarding Bonseok, Chris, Jennifer, Todd and Scott. He gave an eloquent and heartfelt speech, which captured the unique qualities of each of these wonderful people. In a moving tribute following his speech, members of the River Edge Volunteer Fire Department escorted the families into the garden to the strains of the choir singing *America the Beautiful*. The opening of the garden to the general public and a reception followed the families' private viewing.

KEYNOTE SPEECH BY CREIGHTON DRURY

Good afternoon everyone!

As you have probably noticed– I am not a politician, nor a religious leader, nor a world renowned speaker. I am here today simply because of a common bond that we all share - River Edge, New Jersey. I share with many of you the bond of being raised here in River Edge, of having raised my own family in River Edge and of presently living in this wonderful town. Today I represent you, I speak for you! And I can't tell you how humbled I am to have this extraordinary privilege. You see today is not about politics – it is not about religious beliefs – and it is not about some motivational speech. Quite simply – today is about a community which has chosen to express its grief – its compassion – its empathy – its admiration – its love - to the five families who have experienced the extreme loss of their loved one. Today is also about a celebration because today we celebrate the remarkable lives of five beautiful people.

If you were raised in River Edge, as many of us were, you may reflect on the fact that our town doesn't look the same as it did years ago – retail stores have changed ownership, buildings have changed physically, grocery stores have come and gone, banks have changed names and locations, even some of our houses of worship have undergone architectural changes, our recreational areas and schools as well. The only constant in our community – the only thing unchangeable is fortunately what makes River Edge – River Edge – and that is you the people. We are a community of people who care about one another – who care about our children – who look out for each other in the most positive way. And so when neighbors hurt – we all hurt – when neighbors suffer – we all suffer – when neighbors weep – we all weep and when neighbors grieve for the loss of loved ones – we all grieve.

Those of us who grew up in this wonderful community are aware of the many chapters of history that have caused this community to come together – either in celebration or in grief. We have known the scars of war and like other communities we have experienced the loss of those who volunteered to defend our country and paid the ultimate price for that freedom we all cherish and enjoy today. We wept when we lost neighbors, we wept when we lost friends, we wept when we lost fathers, sons, mothers and daughters to these horrible events we call war. Our community is no stranger to these tragedies.

But what happened four years ago – what happened to this nation – to this metropolitan area - to our community of River Edge – to our neighbors and friends – was something that this town could never have anticipated. The loss was unreal - the pain unbearable – the words of comfort fleeting. We were immediately confronted with our own powerlessness and the question of how to begin, as a community, to express our heartfelt sorrow to the families of Scott, Todd, Jen, Chris and Bonseok. How could we possibly

alleviate their pain? But we quickly learned that the reality is that we can't and we shouldn't. The hearts of these families have the right and the need to mourn. But there was something that we could do and so, after two years of planning, we as a community will now do our best to preserve forever the memory of five wonderful residents of our community.

Mitch Alboum wrote a novel entitled, "The Five People You Meet in Heaven." The five people that we honor today are five individuals, living now in Heaven, who lived ordinary lives in extraordinary ways.

Did you know them?

Scott? Todd? Jen? Chris? Bonseok?

Let's visit with them, shall we?

Just for a few moments – this is, of course, their day.

11

BONSEOK KOO

I'd like to speak to you of a young man named Bonseok - Bonseok Koo. Born on February 1, 1959, Bonseok was 42 in 2001.

Adapting to life in the United States was not an easy task for Bonseok, his wife Yunho Cho, and his daughters Jenny and Clara. Fortunately, Bonseok chose River Edge as his home away from home and this decision certainly helped his family to ease the transition from his home country of Korea.

Bonseok was the United States Branch Manager of LG Insurance Company, which has its base in Seoul, Korea. Bonseok knew the meaning of hard work and was usually the first one at the office, which was located on the 84th floor of One World Trade Center. Bonseok had exceptional business skills and was a talented negotiator. It was this skill that helped him to rise quickly in the Korean insurance market. His knowledge of the European insurance market was enhanced when he worked at his company's London office.

But Bonseok wasn't all business. After work he often socialized with his colleagues and staff, enjoying the Korean restaurants located in the garment district of Manhattan. He was a man who cared about his employees and treated them with the utmost respect and dignity. Besides his love for spicy meals, Bonseok enjoyed the game of golf. His busy schedule and prominent position never stopped him from spending time on the golf course or more importantly, with his wife and two daughters at home in River Edge. Helping Jenny and Clara with their homework was a special time for Bonseok. As much as Bonseok enjoyed living in River Edge, he ultimately wanted to return to his home in Korea, to Seoul, the company's main office, and, of course, to his mother, whom he missed dearly.

Bonseok Koo was a most successful businessman and world traveler. He was a man who developed the personal touch and was approachable and available to friends and work associates in need. But above all Bonseok was a devoted family man. A loving husband to Yunho Cho and a devoted and cherished father to Jenny and Clara, his legacy will live on in the family he loved so much.

Yunho Cho, Jenny and Clara, family and friends, know so much more about Bonseok's legacy. They will keep it alive. Memorial Gardens, we believe, will do the same.

CHRISTOPHER ALLINGHAM

I'd like to speak to you of a young man named Chris – Chris Allingham. Born on October 6, 1964, Chris was 36 in 2001.

Raised in Holmdel, New Jersey, Chris graduated with a degree in business from St. Peter's College in Jersey City. After graduation the fast paced life of the New York City business world proved to be the perfect place for Chris's skills. He loved his work. He thrived on pressure. He exuded confidence. Yet at the end of the day, the place he always wanted to be was home with Donna and their two boys, Christopher and Kyle.

Chris was a passionate Giants fan and his favorite pastime was to set up his tailgating party with all the trimmings on game day. Being with family and friends was wonderful but having his two sons, Christopher and Kyle with him, made everything complete.

Chris was truly a devoted father who was involved with his boys in their sports activities including coaching Little League. The Allingham front yard was practically designated a River Edge ball field because it was here that Chris would spend endless hours playing with his sons. Letters from neighbors consistently referred to their memories of watching Chris on the front lawn enthusiastically enjoying every moment with the boys. What the neighbors couldn't see was that the outside activity was only a reflection of what was going on inside the Allingham home. Chris would arrive home in a whirlwind and loved to rile up Christopher and Kyle. Donna smiles recalling the laughter and noise surrounding wrestling matches, games of hide and seek and other activities that demonstrated this unique bond between a father and his sons. When many fathers were trying to unwind on Saturday mornings, Chris would rise early and whisk the boys away to the park. Often he would drive them to Hoboken to savor firsthand the taste of a good cheese steak lunch.

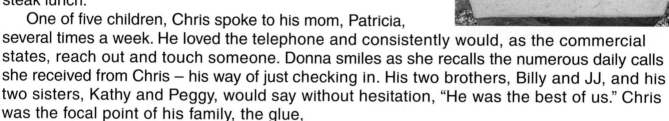

One of five children, Chris spoke to his mom, Patricia, several times a week. He loved the telephone and consistently would, as the commercial states, reach out and touch someone. Donna smiles as she recalls the numerous daily calls she received from Chris – his way of just checking in. His two brothers, Billy and JJ, and his two sisters, Kathy and Peggy, would say without hesitation, "He was the best of us." Chris was the focal point of his family, the glue, the mediator, the one who made sure the family stayed in touch, no matter the distance, no matter the time.

Chris loved to work outside on his River Edge estate. A leaf could barely touch the ground before Chris was ready to blow it aside. He loved his home, he loved to chat with neighbors, and he loved to give back to his community, serving on the Traffic and Safety Committee for several years. River Edge, Bergen County, was gradually winning over the Monmouth County boy.

There are so many beautiful memories that Donna has with Chris – vacations on Cape Cod, time spent with family and friends, precious times spent alone with each other. But in the end the memory that she misses the most is that of Chris bursting in the door at the end of the day. Perhaps that's the greatest compliment that can be given to Chris - he always put his family first. His love for Donna, Christopher, and Kyle is the heart of his legacy. By the way, if you search the audience you won't find Christopher or Kyle here today. At this moment they are at Giants Stadium, carrying on a family tradition for someone they will never forget. Chris's wife, Donna, his sons, Christopher and Kyle, his parents William and Patricia, his two sisters, Kathy and Peggy, his two brothers, Billy and JJ, his family and friends, know so much more about Chris's legacy. They will keep it alive. Memorial Gardens, we believe, will do the same.

JENNIFER LOUISE FIALKO

I'd like to speak to you of a young woman named Jen – Jen Fialko. Born on October, 13th 1971, Jen was 29 in 2001.

Jen was an outstanding athlete at River Dell High School, co-captain of the varsity softball and field hockey teams. And although you saw her name in print and marveled at her athletic ability, you probably didn't read about the thoughts of her coaches and teammates regarding Jen - her sense of humor, her sensitivity to others, her willingness to go the extra mile for those in need, her strength of character, her sense of self that reflected wisdom and understanding far beyond her years.

The vacation years with her family in New Hampshire set the stage for every imaginable form of water skiing and created within Jen a thirst for adventure that included deep sea diving, motorcycling and a special love for boating on Lake Winnipesaukee. But it was on the dock of the family home that Jen would have her favorite memories. It was here that Jen bonded with her brother Andrew, here where she shared with him how she found the man of her life, David. It was here that she enjoyed family reunions with special uncles, aunts and cousins. It was here that Jen had spent seven wonderful summers with her special friend and grandmother, Sally.

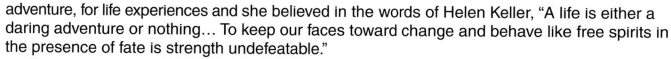

Jen graduated a sociology major from the University of New Hampshire, with a minor in Spanish. Jen had the same effect on her sorority sisters in college as she did on her River Dell teammates. They simply loved her.

Jen loved to travel! She had visited more countries than most of us will visit in a lifetime. She had this thirst for adventure, for life experiences and she believed in the words of Helen Keller, "A life is either a daring adventure or nothing... To keep our faces toward change and behave like free spirits in the presence of fate is strength undefeatable."

To Jen, life was an exciting journey of caring for others and for developing insight into her spirituality. She was thirsty for knowledge and never wasted time in front of the TV. There was too much to learn, too much to explore, too many problems in the world that needed resolution. Jen was a sponge for learning. She would be so pleased that this garden shares the same grounds as the River Edge Library.

Jen was a positive thinker – one who always saw the glass as half full – not half empty. Life's obstacles and struggles demonstrated her belief in the eternal plan. She loved a challenge and the bigger it was the greater her resolve to overcome it and to grow from the experience. Obstacles that would seem insurmountable to most of us, simply helped to manifest her remarkable courage.

Jen loved quotes! Such as: "You're worthy without any proof" or, "Love lives here." Her parents, Evelyn and Bob, have saved many of her famous quotes. Jen also loved to leave little post-it messages around such as the one for her Mom which read, "Mom, smile, I love you. Never forget that. Jennifer."

Both parents remember Jen as someone who snatched life and always took the road less traveled by. She was always there for others and letters still come in, often from people in other countries, describing in detail how Jen had helped them through tough times or how she had such a powerful impact on their lives. Jen's legacy lives on in all of those people that she reached out to help.

Jen's parents, Evelyn and Bob, her brother Andrew, her dearest friend David, her grandmother Sally, her family and friends know so much more about Jen's legacy. They will keep it alive. Memorial Gardens, we believe, will do the same

TODD OUIDA

I'd like to speak to you of a young man named Todd – Todd Ouida. Born on May 18th, 1976, Todd was 25 in 2001.

Todd could have been a walking advertisement for River Edge. He simply loved River Edge. He loved the schools he attended and he loved to participate in the recreational programs each summer held at Memorial Park. Come to think of it – there was nothing that Todd didn't love about this town. The friends he made growing up remained close to Todd throughout the college years and the two years that followed. They all realized that Todd was someone special – someone who knew the true meaning of friendship – someone who always would be there for them. And he was.

Todd learned early in life that when obstacles or problems arise, it is necessary to face them head on and conquer them rather than settling for the easy solution of accepting less. This became Todd's philosophy of life. So if he had to work harder to make the River Dell Varsity football team – so be it. Imagine the pride of his family and friends to see Todd become the starting defensive back in his senior year. The recollection of his first interception is etched forever in the Ouida family memory.

So it was certainly no surprise that Todd decided to reach for the stars and apply to the University of Michigan, one of the top schools in the nation. You guessed it - he was accepted. He loved those Michigan football games and fraternity life with his friends was most memorable. Todd's major was Psychology and this choice probably related to his love for children that began when he spent summers as a lifeguard. Todd had a special gift for relating to children, often drawing on his own childhood experiences to establish a meaningful connection. Following Todd's graduation he embarked on a successful career with his brother, Jordan, at Cantor Fitzgerald. He loved his job and worked there for two years.

His love for his big sister Amy was special and when he was asked to be the godfather to her baby Ashley he became ecstatic. No gift could surpass this and Ashley became the love of his life. He once wrote: "To Ashley, the most important person in my life." His friends recognizing this special relationship collectively bought a bond for Ashley, to be used for having fun following her final year of college - just something that Todd would have done.

One of Todd's shining moments came during his toast at his brother Jordan's wedding. If you had the privilege of being there or watching the video, you would have thought that Todd could have passed for a handsome actor, or a comedian, but his expression of admiration and respect for his role model, Jordan, left everyone speechless. His sense of humor was known to all and his Mom, Andrea, smiles as she recalls one particular e-mail, a one-liner which just left her in stitches. Herb's recollections include many wonderful Saturdays with Todd each year at Yankee Stadium, cheering for Todd's favorite team.

Perhaps the best way to summarize Todd is through his own words, written in his essay to the University of Michigan before admission, "I realized that the time a person wants to give up, is the time when it is imperative for that person to fight the hardest. I learned that with a family a person can overcome anything. And I discovered no matter how big the person is on the outside (for I am only 5'5" tall) that the size of the heart is always going to be more important." Todd has proven that to be true!

His parents, Andrea and Herb, his brother Jordan and his sister Amy, their spouses Heather and Alex, his family and friends know so much more about Todd's legacy. They will keep it alive. Memorial Gardens, we believe, will do the same.

SCOTT W. ROHNER

I'd like to speak to you of a young man named Scott – Scott Rohner. Born on March 23, 1979, Scott was 22 in 2001.

If Hollywood ever wanted to make a movie about an All-American kid – you know the type – the boy who would try anything, risk everything, play every possible game imaginable, wrestle in the dirt and then when he caught the eye of his mother would just flash the greatest smile, - after a thousand casting sessions, looking for the perfect one to play the role – they'd just have to choose Scott. He seemed to capture what childhood should be like for all boys.

Scott excelled at every sport. When he himself wasn't playing, he would watch his older brothers' and his sisters' ballgames, anticipating his own moment to shine - and shine he did. As captain of the River Dell basketball and football teams, Scott left his mark on not only the athletic program but most importantly on his coaches and teammates who respected him for his commitment, unselfish nature and his genuine concern for others. Scott left this same impression on his friends and teammates at Hobart College where Scott continued his athletic talent on the basketball court and the football field. As one teammate stated in a tribute to Scott, "He was a leader and a friend who will be missed by many. When the bell goes off before the football games, Scott is the one I will think of."

Scott had a phenomenal work ethic. As soon as the opportunity arose – Scott was there – to deliver newspapers, to baby-sit, to caddy at Ridgewood Country Club. In college while other students took advantage of spring or winter break to de-stress, Scott would work. Cold weather, hot weather, he worked - and never complained.

Scott had a saying that he used in high school to his teammates, "Step up and play!" It was his way of challenging others to set high standards and to never quit. He never wanted to outdo others but only to motivate himself to do better. Step up and play – it was the way he lived his life.

His major in economics, and his generous personality and that gracious smile, helped to prepare him for his job with Cantor Fitzgerald. Instead of entertaining his clients with drinks after work, Scott would play three-on-three basketball with them - something he always enjoyed playing with his three brothers in Hoboken. The world of Hoboken and New York City was the perfect place for Scott's initiation to the workforce.

Throughout his young life he remained the charming, generous, funny, intelligent, unselfish and compassionate person who touched the lives of all he met. Tributes from friends continue to pour in stating how Scott had touched their lives, how his laughter is missed and how life will never be the same without him.

Kathy and Ron don't hesitate to say that Scott was and is special. They feel his presence all the time and draw strength from their children and the great friends that were devoted to Scott and still keep his memory alive in so many creative ways.

One of his friends wrote, "Scott - twenty-two, exceptional, an angel among us … who felt the idealism of youth, the unconditional love of family, and a responsibility to make the world a better place." Scott's legacy will emphatically state - that he did.

Scott's parents, Kathy and Ron, his sisters, Kristen and Katie, his brothers, Mike, Steven, and Tom, his family and friends, know so much more about Scott's legacy. They will keep it alive. Memorial Gardens, we believe, will do the same.

Abraham Lincoln once said, "In the end it's not the years in your life that count. It's the life in your years."

These five people packed into their young lives what most of us could only dream of. They didn't waste a second and to quote the famous Latin phrase, Carpe Diem, they seized every moment that was given to them and they explored all the opportunities that came their way.

Throughout all of their stories there are so many qualities that they had in common. There were the concrete successes of athleticism, education, career accomplishments. But it was the human qualities that struck me the most. All possessed great smiles and had a wonderful sense of humor. They all were compassionate individuals who saw the good in others, recognized the importance of family, were generous, loved work, were non-judgmental, had positive attitudes and above all were just kind and loving people. They all demonstrated a maturity far beyond their years. They chose to be players in life. They danced their way through this journey and they danced their way into the hearts of all who were privileged to have known them.

During my cherished conversations with family members, different wishes were expressed – the wish for one last dance – one last conversation – one last hug. But words were also articulated about how the Memorial Gardens now gives them a place to go, to reflect, and to remember their loved one. As one parent said, reflecting the sentiment of all the families, "We didn't go to the town and request this. The people of River Edge and the Committee, who worked so hard on this project, generously have given us a gift that is just priceless."

And so today we come together as a community - to dedicate this memorial as a symbolism of our grief - to express in the most reverent way the admiration we have for the families who have experienced such painful loss and who have demonstrated for all of us what courage and strength are all about – but most of all to honor the memory of those whose lives were cut short on September 11th, 2001.

There is a famous Irish song with the following verse, "In my memory I will always see, the town that I have loved so well." From this day forth all of our recollections of River Edge will echo that verse because our memories will not be of stores and landmarks that have come and gone but rather of this Memorial Garden and the five inspirational people whom we honor today.

We all will pass these Memorial Gardens often in our future days. Generations to come will do likewise. And we will easily be caught up with daily distractions and concerns – but if we allow ourselves to listen, often this beautiful memorial will call to us – and remind us –of Scott – of Todd – of Jen – of Chris - of Bonseok. It will remind us of their contributions to River Edge – of their smiles – of their gifts and of the special way they have touched the lives of all of us.

And so when you pass – by yourself – with your spouse - with your children – your grandchildren – maybe even great-grandchildren – smile as you pass – think of them fondly –reflect on their legacy – stop in to stroll and say a silent prayer and remember how lucky we all are for this town and the gift we all are to one another. It is what they – Scott, Todd, Jen, Chris and Bonseok, would want us to do. Their legacy lives on in all of us who are charged with telling their story and remembering the gift they were and are to this community we all call home.

Creighton Drury

23

Acknowledgements

Thank you to all who have given so generously in the creation of this memorial,
with special thanks to:

River Edge Free Public Library
Board of Trustees:
George Dunphey, President
Patricia Dalton
Ronald Hardiman
William Lins
Mary Kay McHugh
George Riley
Winifred Wunschel

Daragh O'Connor, Library Director
River Edge Public Library Staff

Borough of River Edge:
Mayor Margaret Falahee Watkins

River Edge Borough Council:
Council President Mary Anne O'Connell Hone
Councilman John Felice
Councilwoman Esther Fletcher
Councilman John B. Higgins
Councilman Christian J. Lau
Councilman Thomas Smith

Alan P. Negreann, Borough Administrator
William R. Lindsley, Esq., Borough Attorney
Denise A. Dondiego, Borough Clerk
Staff of Borough Hall

Acknowledgements (cont.)

River Edge Police Department

River Edge Volunteer Fire Department

River Edge Department of Public Works

River Edge Beautification Committee

River Edge Chamber of Commerce

River Edge Cultural Center

Interfaith Choir, directed by Gloria Norton

Garden Development

Conceptual Design:
Keehn Landscape Contractors Incorporated
Charles Keehn, President
Patrick A. Smith, Landscape Designer

Construction Documents & Supervision:
Costa Engineering
Robert L. Costa, President
Christopher Carry, Field Inspector

Construction:
Let It Grow Incorporated
Paul T. Imbarrato, President
Paul E. Papapetrou, Project Manager

Memorial Book
Don Bonner, design, layout, photography
Dr. Joseph Friedlander & Tom McCarthy, photography

Jennifer

Todd

Bonseok

Scott

Chris

Contributors to the 9/11 Memorial Gardens

Unless otherwise noted, all contributors are from the town of River Edge

Contributors over $1,000.00

Christopher E. Allingham Family Memorial Trust, Holmdel, NJ
William Allingham Jr. & James Allingham

Cititech Services Incorporated, North Bergen, NJ
Jorge & Barbara Teran, Jackson Township, NJ

DeLoach Paving, Clifton, NJ
David DeLoach & Family

Andrew Fialko

Robert & Evelyn Fialko

Keene Landscape Contractors, Hackensack, NJ
Charles & Maryanne Keehn, Paramus, NJ

Herbert & Andrea Ouida

Frances & George Riley

River Edge Diner & Restaurant
Steven Siderias & Alex Alexandris

Ronald & Katherine Rohner

Sanducci's Trattoria
Anthony & Lisa DeMiglio

Alan Spiniello, Esq., Hackensack, NJ

Topkote Refinishing, Paramus, NJ
Robert Alexander & Family

Sarah Zick

Contributors of $500.00 to $999.00

Aplex Air Conditioning and Refrigeration
Barry Hoaire, Little Falls, NJ

Thomas Barrett, Esq.

Saleverio Cereste Esq.

James & Elizabeth Conway

Costa Engineering, Hackensack, NJ
Robert Costa Family

John & Regina Higgins

Yun H Koo-Cho, Cresskill, NJ

Lanni Appliances, Rutherford, NJ
Edward Lanni & Family

Let It Grow Incorporated, Paul Imbarrato

Richard & Laura McDermott, Vero Beach, FL

Nigito Realty Company, The Nigito Family

Resolution Properties of New Hampshire,
Mark & Kay Henry, North Andover, MA

T & T Masonry, Samuel Tait, Paterson, NJ

Veterans of Foreign Wars, Caldroney Klaiber Frost Post 876

W.A.T. What A Tee Inc., Hackensack, NJ
Harry Poulis, Haworth, NJ

Donald & Ana Zick, West Barnstable, MA

Robert Zick Family

Russ Zick, Lynn Gamble &
Family, Denver, CO

Contributors of $250.00 to $499.00

Aon Risk Services Incorporated, New York, NY

Cherry Hill Student Council

Conklin Insurance Company, Hackensack,
Gerard Quinn, Oradell, NJ

Ludwig Plumbing & Heating, Joseph Ludwig, Haworth, NJ

McDonald's Restaurant, Robert Dunham

Quality Cooling Corporation,
Joseph & Carol Pignatelli, Ho-Ho-Kus, NJ

Christopher & Jacqueline Riley, Hasbrouck Heights, NJ

Keith & Lydia Riley, Ho-Ho-Kus, NJ

Contributors of $100.00 to $249.00

Roger & Phyllis Angelo
Allan & Cheryl Baer
James & Jennifer Bieber
David Bihl, Waterford, NJ
Jean Brodowicz
Thomas & Maureen Cameron, Oradell, NJ
Christopher & Elizabeth Caruso
Christine Valmy Day Spa, Mary Monemuro
Joseph Colella, Esq.
Paul & Barbara Conly Jr., North Plainfield, NJ
John & Ann Curley
Jane Dalton
John & Patricia Dalton
Vincent Damore
Jonathan & Nancy Davis
Delford Flowers, Randi Duffie
Natalie Dengler
Mary Donohue
Creighton & Valerie Drury
George & Helen Dunphey
Edwin L. Morse Incorporated, Edwin L. Morse, Wareham, MA
Joseph Friedlander, MD
Margaret Garofalo
Gary's All American Heating and Cooling, Gary Hotko
Jack & Janet George
Robert & Joyce Gorman
Ronald & Peggy Hardiman
Kevin & Patricia Hart
Jay's Pharmacy,
Nicholas & Joyce Ignazzi
Wun Ye Jiu & Richard Lee
William Kalosieh
Michael & Jacqueline Kelly
Irfan Kirimca
Lorraine & Julia Knapp
Patricia O'Boyle Kost
Robert & Risa Louda

Contributors of $100.00 to $249.00

Denise Lynch, Rockville Center, NY
John & Geraldine Maiolo
Paul & Jean Marino
Michael Marion
Tom & Ann McCarthy
Richard & Allison McDermott, Darien, CT
Allen & Helen Meccia
Richard & Maureen Mehrman
Robert & Jane O'Connell
Daragh O'Connor & Tammy Valentine
Eileen O'Connor
John & Marian O'Neill
Justin Osterman
Palmer Brothers, Bruce & David Palmer
Michael & Jo-Anne Pecoraro
Leonardo & Olga Pimentel
PNC Bank
Policemen's Benevolent Association
of River Edge, Local 201
Kenneth & Erica Quinn
River Edge Dry Cleaners, Patty Shin
River Edge Republican Campaign Committee
Roosevelt School PTO
Albert & Audrey Ruhlmann, Jr.
Bruce & Stephanie Safro
Shirley Schuyler
Thomas & Marie Smith
John & Joan Sullivan
Patricia Tamargo
Fritz & Renate Thiermann
Tony's Cleaners, Anthony Isaga
Peter & Theresa Vanderbeck
Russell & Noreen Van Wetering
Paul & Jo Ann Vlacancich, Struthers, OH
Wetlands Incorporated, Christine Imbarrato
Linda Wollerman
Woman's Club of River Edge

Contributors of $50.00 to $99.00

A.R.S. Enterprises
Robert & Hilma Albrecht
American Legion Auxiliary Unit 226
Anderson-Bernard Agency Incorporated
Jose Arguelles
Andrew & Mary Berg
Bergen Batting Center, David Schwartz
Jose Branco
Lloyd Breslin
Charles & Patricia Brunje
Built-Well Home Improvements
E. Scott & Mary Burke, East Weymouth, MA
Stephen & Patricia Cali
James & Elaine Campbell
Brenda Canal, Oradell, NJ
Vincent & Helen Cassel
Castle Builders, Craig Anderson
John & Doris Chatellier
Mary Clark
Robert & Maxine Cole
Matthew & Philomena Connell
Michael & Joan Curley
William & Jane Daly
DanMar Press, Daniel Stenchever,
Hackensack, NJ
Emilio & Elizabeth Dellapenta
Theresa DeLorenzo
Dinallo's Restaurant, Robert Dinallo
Timothy & Ann Duggan
Gary Dunlop
Hagop Jack & Jeanette Ekizian
Donald & Donna Fanelli
Ellen Farmer
Joan Feeley
John & Janet Felice
Nathan Fink Esq., Oradell, NJ
Patrick & Esther Fletcher
Jane Galgoci, Port Matilda, PA
Thomas & Mary Gannon
Peter & Elaine Gibbons
Vincent & Mary Ann Guiliano
Moonseong & Miseon Heo

Contributors of $50.00 to $99.00

Christopher & Lisa Herrick
Snowden & Marie Herrick
Mary Anne O'Connell Hone
James & Victoria Horner
Linda Hurlburt
Chris Ilg
Stephen Ip
Tadashi & Itsuko Ishiguro
Sharon Jaffee
Maureen Janik
Edward & Gloria Jentz
Matthew & Karen Judge
Perry & Frances Kasturas
Denise Kehoe
Leslie & Linda Klein
Knights of Columbus Council 5015
Joseph & Mary Lennox
Stephen Levine, DDS
William & Irene Lindlsey
Dervis & Cathleen Magistre
Margaret & Cathleen Mahoney
Abraham & Silva Manjikian
Barbara McDonnell
Linell McDonough
Joseph & Michael McFadden
Philip & Julie McGarry
Michael & Elizabeth McLaughlin
Peter & Peggy McLoughlin, Newtonville, MA
Thomas & Dolores Meehan
Stuart & Andrea Meher
Richard Mehrman PE
Gunnar & Susan Mengers
Gertrude Miller
Richard & Mary Miller
Brian & Kathleen Mitchell
Patrick Mitchell
Anthony & Margaret Molesi
Rogert & Marilyn Neagle
New Nail Art, Kelly Lee
New Jersey Decorators Exchange,
David Greenberg
Brenda Nix
Neville Ottmann

Contributors of $50.00 to $99.00

Carlo & Alyssa Rebosio
Richard Reinstein
Robert & Dorothy Roane
John & Deborah Rossi
Jon Rothschild, C.P.A.
Arthur & Marjorie Sandberg
Nicolo & Jean Scariano
Robert & Mary Schmand
Arthur & Dolores Schmitt
Alice & Alvah Scott
Michael & Rosemarie Short
Allison Shreffler
Specialty Sports Productions/SSP, Ron Sticco
Louise Spencer
Sylvester Chiropractic Center,
Robert Sylvester Family
Timothy J. Walker Plumbing & Heating
David & Jane Triglia
Nicholas & Claire Valvano
Thomas Wall, Esq., Edgewater, NJ
William & Margaret Watkins
Willard & JoAnn Wilson
James & Bridgette Woods Jr.
Mary Ellen Wyllie

Contributors up to $50.00

AARP Chapter #2131 of River Edge
Gaylord & Norma Adams
Michael & Tina Alfis
Stacey Anastos
Eloise Andersen
Elizabeth Anievas
Marcia Archibald
Richard Arida
Christine Armstrong
Floyd & Zenith Aronow
Donna Auriemma
Eileen Austin
Michael & Mary Azarian
John Backes
Stanley Bagnasco

Stephen & Melissa Bailey
Carol Ann Barba
Evelyn & Lori Baronian
John & Kathleen Barrett
Susan Barrise
Margaret Barry
Renzo Barto
Frank & Karen Bayersdorfer
Linda Bayreuther
Thomas & Linda Behrens
Shelley Benjamin
William & Eleanor Bennett
Grant & Susan Bergman
Martin & Phyllis Besen
Richard & Gomattie Birnbaum

Contributors up to $50.00

Bernard & Karen Blick
Leonard & Linda Bogan
Armand & Joan Bogosian
Vincent & Patricia Bossone
Maryanna & Valarie Bove
John & Mariann Bradley
Denis & Dorothy Brauchle
Frank Breitbarth
Theresa Brielmaier
Reid & Maria Brockmeier
Joseph Brooks
Adria Brown
Robert & Cathy Bucchieri
John & Mary Buckley
Ruth Biheller & Rachel Bunin
Janet Buono
E. Scott & Mary Burke
Raymond & Gail Buttenbaum
Hamlet Campagna
Paul Campanelli
William & Elizabeth Campbell
John & Josephine Campo
Timothy & Adrienne Capasso
Barbara Cappelli
Stamatia Carabos
William & Anna Caruso
Roy & Marcia Caspe
Karla Cerelli & James Leahy
Denise Chavanne
Scott & Doris Cisternino
John & Susan Claehsen
Bianca Claps
Alvin & Helen Clark
Charles & Patricia Cochran
Carol Cocco
Irving & Lila Cohen
Irwin & Douglas Cohen
Peter & Neila Cohen
Peter & Ann Colucio
David & Patricia Comiso
David & Jeanne Connors, New York, NY
William & Barbara Connors
Lyle J. Cookson
William & Lillian Corcoran
Nicholas & Rosemary Costabile
James Coursen
Celia Crehan
Patrick & Mary Crehan
Frederick Croes, Concord, NH

Lawrence & Katherine Croes,
Alton Bay, NH
Crown Trophy, Chuck Hedbavny
Sahid & Deborah Dahabsu
Walter & Maryann Dalbey
Donna D'Aloisio
Richard & Filomena D'Aloisio
Kevin & Mary Daly
Dante's, Joseph Pignatelli Jr.
Gerard & Ellen Davino
Eileen Davis
Victor & Sheila DeCosmis
John & Flora Delmour
Jeffrey & Cecelia DelPrete
Derek DePol
Colleen DeSanctis
Robert Devlin
Rosalinda Diaz
Joseph & Eileen Di Cara
Angelina Di Marco
William & Norma Dittrich
Marc Dodge
Alan & Constance Doerner
Robert & Denise Dondiego
David & Teresa Donohue
James & June Donohue
Ian & Mary Doris
Joseph & Bernice Drapkin
Ann Drossman
Dunkin Donuts, Ramila Palet
Eugene & Rosemary Dunton
Grace Durdunas
James Duthie
Evelyn Dykes
Joseph & Theresa Esposito
John & Leela Evancho
Wormok Kim Evans
Robert & Bridgette Falanga
Deborah Fantini-Martinez & Angel Martinez
Helen Fazio
George & Marian Fernandez
Alan & Frieda Finkelstein
Thomas & Kathleen Flynn
Christine Foley
Mary Foody
David & Dina Fried
Stephen & Edythe Fried
Estelle Friedberg
Anahid Fritsche

Contributors up to $50.00

Fanny Fuentes
Selwyn Fung
Frank & Geraldine Garcia
Douglas Garofalo
Jack Garoyan
Raymond & Susan Gehringer
Thomas & Thoedora Gernegliaro
James & Donna Giannisis
David & Karen Glass
Stephen & Linda Goldberg
Frederick & Christine Gonnerman
Myra Good
Christine Goodelman
Eric & Syma Goodman
Norma Gottlieb
Robert Graillat
Raymond & Nancy Gramkow
Stephen & Dawn Grenz
Beatrice Gross
Glenn & Lara Gutin
Scott Hacker & Karen Negris
Margaret Haggerty
Roger & Madeleine Hall
Mary Hallahan
John & Janet Hamalian
Irene Harold
Robert Hart
Arthur & Carolyn Harvey
Kan He & Zheng Guan
Albert Hein
Grace Heuber & Jean Nobbs
Carmen Higgins
Roy & Henie Horton
Michael & Ann Hroncich
Catherine Hughes
Steven & Janice Insler
Ferdinand Iucci
Anthony & Mary Izzo
Lucia Jaklitsch
Charles Jascheck Jr.
Daniel & Nanette Jiji
William & Jacqueline Johnson
Vladimir & Valeria Jornitski
Rex & Carin Karyshyn
Sally Katz
Joachim & Phyllis Kaufhold
Barry & Brooke Kaye
John & Virginia Kehoe
Lillian Kehoe

John & Mary Kelly
Joseph & Elene Kennelly
Marion Kennelly
Mary Jane Kennelly
Vincent & Colleen Kiely
Helen Kinoian
Arthur & Mary Kay Klepper
Bart & Beverly Klim
Robert Kornhaber & Genia Peterson
John & Belida Krivy
Thomas & Dorothy Kroll
Eiko Kubo
Richard & Amy Kulesza
Joseph & Ava Kulin
Spencer & Sophia Kuo
Thomas & Debra Kyritz
Carol Lamendola
Michael & Jessica Lamolino
Edward & Sheila Lane
David & Arlene Lapidos
Maurice & Doris Lavigne
Dennis & Ivetty Lebright
Joseph & Diane Lefkowitz
Ruth Leiman
James & Renee Lemakos
Elaine Levine
Robert & Edith Levine
James & Claudia Levis
Juliana & Eugenij Lezaja
James & Elizabeth Licata
Patricia Liddell
Jungbin Lim & Sung Dae Cho
Carl & Anita Lindke
Lysiane Linoir
William & Gladys Lins
Leslie & Caroline Lippencott
Catherine Lomascola
Joseph Lombardi
Barbara & Maryann Longobardo
Robert & Esther Lorbeer
Harold & Fran Lowenfels
Keith & Doreen Luca
John & Joann Lucey
Mary Mackin
Carmine & Deborah Maddalena
Henry & Carol Mah
Donald & Elizabeth Maher
Carol Malle
Edward & Alice Malone

Contributors up to $50.00

Lillian Mandell
Jamie Marcella
Frances Marcellus
Janet Marcus
Madeline Maresca
Patricia Marotti
Douglas & Dorothy Martin
James & Judith Martin
The Martin Family
Kathy Massa
Elvira Matichka
Frederick & Dorothy May
Dveyra Mayzel & Lyubov Funshteyn
Fanya Mayzel & Lyubov Funshteyn
Mazzone's Pizzeria & Restaurant
John & Jill McCabe
Mary McCarthy
Walter McColl
Randall & Thyra McCormack
Francis & Ann McDonnell
John McDonnell
Michael & Marie McDonough
Leo & Sandra McGarry
Mary Ellen McHugh-Seidel
Kevin & Anne McKegney
Christopher McKenna
Marguerite McMahon
Janet McMullun
Marie Meehan
Edward & Alice Melone
John & Eleanor Messersmith
Michael & Diane Miello
Stanley & Dorothy Mikolajczyk
Arlene Miller
Luigi & Lisa Milordo
Marco & Maria Minervini
Rose Pauline & Rose Anne Minnich
Karl & Ann Mock
Eric Model, Esq.
Audrey Camelet Moles
Michael & Martha Moles
Vincente & Alma Molina
Ruth Monahan
Agnes Montemurro
Rosemarie Monteverde
Janice Ann Morris
June Morris
Carl & Karen Morrow
Harold Mudge

Laurel Mudrick
William & Marie Munson
Myrna Muntner
Kevin & Colleen Murrell
Marian Murrin
Diane Naprstek
Raymond & Mary Ng
Jon & Gloria Norton
Robert Nyman
Gladys O'Brian & Marilyn Good
Maura O'Brien
James & Mary O'Donnell
Madeline O'Donnell
Conceicao Ogawa
Jo Ognibene
John & Rebecca Ohanesian
Vasken & Regina Ohanyan
Therese O'Hara
Carl & Laraine Olson
John & Teresa Orth
Joan Osterlof
Raymond & Karen Pace
Richard & Elaine Paolillo
Seongkoo Park
Antoinette Pasqualicchio
Scott & Maria Pauli
William & Genevieve Percival
Michael & Mary Pesce
Joseph & Danielle Picone
Joseph & Dolores Picone
Richard & Susan Pike
Judith Whitmore Poa
Harold & Urve Pohi
Jerome & Miriam Preis
John & Jennie Psihoules
Graciela Pushaw
Francis & Sharon Quara
Robert & Hyacinth Quinn
Evergistro & Anna Ramos
Richard & Sharon Raska
Seymour & Judith Ratner
Anna Ricca
Robert & Judith Richard
Timothy & Michelle Riecken
Harold & Jeanne Riedel
Victor & Sylvia Rivera
John & Claire Roche
Jeanne Rock
Susan Rodemeyer

Contributors up to $50.00

Nancy Roman
Andrew & Adelia Rosen
Daniel & Claire Rosenbaum
Jonathan & Wendy Rosenoff
Yoshiko Roshida
Wayne & Marie Ross
Samuel & Fay Roth
Adeline Rovegno
Edward Russell
William & Jean Ryan
Kevin & Carolyn Sabella
Jerome & Roseanne Sachs
Sylvia Saladino
Alain & Amy Sanders
Gerald & Nelia Sanzari
John & Barbara Sarafian
Martin & Lucille Sarkisian
Richard & Abby Satel
Albert & Muriel Sauer
Mae Schaffeld
Charles & May Scheck
John & Agnes Schmonsees
Howard & Florence Schneiderman
Elaine Schreier
Steve & Marsha Schlossberg
Ronald Schreiber, Elmwood Park, NJ
William & Mary Schwitter
Kenneth & Linda Scott
Betty Seldin
Brian & Aarthi Seligman
Sol & Claire Seltzer
Shanghai Restaurant, Li Rong Huang
Jack & Elynore Shapiro
George & Maureen Sherger
Klara Sieber
Paul & Lori Sillari
Ruth Simpson
Scott & Jennifer Soiferman
Melvyn & Lillian Solomon
Gregory & Kerry Spano
Richard & Janet Sperling
Yefrem Spravtsev & Irina Poznanskaya
Andrew & Arline Steimle

Ted Stein
Austin & Elyse Steinart
Barbara Steinman
Robert & Patricia Stinziano
Supercuts, Robin Wilters
Judi Sussman
Denis & Kristine Sweeny
Eugene & Margo Tauberman
Robert & Sheri Teunisen
Carol Trabert
Julia Tracey
Denise Thompson
Shigekazu & Masako Uejima
Max & Nilda Ugarte
Susan Usatine
Diane Van Miert
G.L. & Margaret Van Valen
Theresa Van Wetering
John & Diane Velten
Boris & Irina Vertsman
William & Carole Walker Jr.
Bin Yuan & Zhaohui Wang
Michael & Carmenia Wasmer
Kipp & Emily Watson
Gloria Weiss
Martin & Lillian Weinstein
Kyle & Kristina Weldon
Alan & Doris Werner
William & Emily Weierstall
Pil & Kay Whang
Diane Whitcomb
Peggy White
Richard & Mary Wiggins
Joan Winters
Yvonne Wolf
Cynthia Wolstromer
Winifred Wunschel
Philip & Laura Wyks, Oradell, NJ
Michael & Mary Yanich
Alma Yee
Matthew & Arlene Zaolino
Mary Zeigler
James & Patricia Zemaites

*Their legacy lives on in all of us who are charged with tellin[g]
their story and remembering the gift they were and are to
this community we all call home.*

Printed in the United States
by Baker & Taylor Publisher Services